WOULD YOU RATHER?...

fascinating questions to ask your friends!!

By Courtney Balestier

BFF!!

Date a guy who was dumb but hot OR smart but ugly?

Get caught cheating on a test OR cheating on your boyfriend?

Not be able to keep a secret OR not be able to tell a lie?

Edited by Justin Heimberg & David Gomberg

Published by Seven Footer Press
276 Fifth Ave, Suite 301
New York, NY 10001

First Printing, August 2009
10 9 8 7 6 5 4 3 2
© Copyright Justin Heimberg and David Gomberg, 2009
All Rights Reserved

Cover Design by Junko Miyakoshi
Design by Thomas Schirtz

ISBN 978-1-934734-08-7

www.sevenfooterpress.com

Tough Choices

Adults always say you have it easy. Free shelter, simple schedule, nothing to worry about except history tests and whether you want that Frappucino plain or with whipped cream. But being a girl is hard.

You might not be paying a mortgage or working a full-time job, but you still face tough decisions every day: Would you rather date the school's star athlete or the valedictorian? Would you rather have ten casual friends or one BFF? Can I really pull off shiny leggings?

You have just as many choices to make as your grown-up counterparts, and the constant drama of high school can make each decision feel more apocalyptic than the one before it. So what's a girl to do? Well, start with the choices on the following pages. If you can handle those, then you're probably in pretty good shape. And just remember, no matter what anyone says, boys will always be hard to figure out.

Table of Contents

CHAPTER 1

Boys

Boys. Life would be so much easier without them. Then again, what would there be to obsess about? From swoon-worthy to barf-worthy, boys are a fact of life. As if you're not thinking about boys too much already, here are some boy-related quandaries to consider.

Would you rather...

go out with a guy who has really long nose hair

OR

horrendous body odor?

Would you rather...

date the hot-but-jerky captain of the football team

OR

the nerdy-but-nice captain of the chess team?

YOU MUST CHOOSE!

Would you rather your date have...

short hair **OR** shaggy hair?

blue eyes **OR** brown eyes?

money **OR** looks?

YOU MUST CHOOSE!

Would you rather your date have...

contacts **OR** glasses?

bad breath **OR** bad manners?

acne **OR** braces?

Follow-up: What does your ideal date look like?

YOU MUST CHOOSE!

Would you rather...

burp as you're about to be kissed

OR

have Dorito breath when you are kissed?

Would you rather date...

McDreamy **OR** McSteamy?

Michael Phelps **OR** Derek Jeter?

Ryan Gosling **OR** Ryan Reynolds?

YOU MUST CHOOSE!

Boys

5

Would you rather...

have a magical power that made guys turn bright purple every time they lied

OR

a power that made them slap themselves in the face every time they checked out another girl?

YOU MUST CHOOSE!

Would you rather...

your guy brag every detail of your make-out session to his friends

OR

not?

Would you rather...

go with your guy to the same movie as your parents

OR

as your ex and his new girlfriend?

YOU MUST CHOOSE!

Would you rather...

have a date who's too shy to talk

OR

one who won't shut up?

Would you rather...

be asked on a date to McDonald's

OR

a *Battlestar Galactica* marathon?

Follow-up: What's the worst date you've ever had?

YOU MUST CHOOSE!

Would you rather...

be asked on a date to a romantic five-star restaurant in Paris

OR

a seaside meal in Hawaii?

Would you rather...

know what boys are thinking all the time

OR

be able to make them say anything that you want?

YOU MUST CHOOSE!

Would you rather...

every time you see your crush, spontaneously burst into song like in a musical

OR

shoot steam out of your ears like in a cartoon?

YOU MUST CHOOSE!

Would you rather...

marry a tall, average-looking guy

OR

someone who looks like Brad Pitt, but two feet shorter?

Would you rather...

have a reputation as a heavy sweater

OR

a bad kisser?

YOU MUST CHOOSE!

Would you rather...

your guy call you once a month

OR

every five minutes?

Would you rather...

your boyfriend catch you cheating

OR

farting?

YOU MUST CHOOSE!

Would you rather...

date a guy who was dumb but hot **OR** smart but ugly?

super interesting but a terrible kisser **OR** incredibly boring but a fantastic kisser?

someone who constantly makes you laugh but your friends hate **OR** someone who bores you but your friends love?

Boys

YOU MUST CHOOSE!

13

Would you rather...

see your boyfriend hit on your best friend

OR

your sister?

Would you rather...

have the worst first date ever

OR

be stood up?

YOU MUST CHOOSE!

Would you rather...

date a guy who compulsively picked his nose

OR

who took pride in belching the alphabet?

Would you rather...

your boyfriend be able to sing like Justin Timberlake

OR

dance like him?

YOU MUST CHOOSE!

Would you rather...

date a guy who referred to himself in the third person

OR

who referred to himself as "Studs McGee"?

Would you rather...

date a guy who wore leopard-print shirts

OR

who wore socks and sandals?

YOU MUST CHOOSE!

While chatting up a guy as you're walking to class, would you rather...

fall down

OR

throw up?

YOU MUST CHOOSE!

Would you rather...

sprout a face full of zits the day of a date

OR

have explosive diarrhea that lasts 20 minutes during the date?

Would you rather...

be asked out via an ad in the school paper

OR

via the school loudspeaker?

YOU MUST CHOOSE!

Would you rather...

accidentally text the juicy details of your date to—whoops!—your date

OR

to your mom?

Would you rather...

date a guy who is 15 pounds skinnier than you

OR

5 inches shorter than you?

YOU MUST CHOOSE!

Would you rather...

a boy try to win your affection by writing you a song

OR

by painting a picture of you?

Follow-up: What's the most romantic thing anyone ever did for you?

YOU MUST CHOOSE!

Would you rather...

date the star athlete

OR

the valedictorian?

Would you rather...

your date to the homecoming dance show up in a powder blue tux

OR

in leather pants?

YOU MUST CHOOSE!

Would you rather...

be able to know every guy who's looked at your Facebook profile

OR

be able to know how often your crush has looked at it?

YOU MUST CHOOSE!

Would you...

not have a single date all through high school if you'd meet the love of your life in college?

ever ask out a guy in front of all his friends?

sneak out of the house after curfew to go on a date with your crush?

go on a date with someone your parents forbid you to see? How about someone your parents want to set you up with?

YOU MUST CHOOSE!

Would you rather date...

Zac **OR** Corbin?

Drake **OR** Josh?

Chuck **OR** Nate?

YOU MUST CHOOSE!

Would you rather...

have a personal dating coach

OR

a personal fashion coach?

Would you rather...

be asked out by your best guy friend

OR

your best girlfriend's crush?

YOU MUST CHOOSE!

CHAPTER

Celebrities and Pop Culture

The life of a celebrity is full of difficult choices. Drive the Porsche or the Escalade? Buy a diamond necklace or a yacht? Adopt a child from China or Africa? Luckily, we ordinary people can just take it easy and watch from the sidelines. Still, it's fun to imagine...

Would you rather...

have Miley Cyrus's voice

OR

her bank account?

Would you rather...

be a character on *Beverly Hills 90210*

OR

on *Gossip Girl?*

YOU MUST CHOOSE!

If there were a movie made about your life, would you rather it star...

Scarlett Johansson

OR

Megan Fox?

Follow-up: If you could choose anyone, who would you want cast as you?

YOU MUST CHOOSE!

Would you rather...

fight Gisele for Tom Brady

OR

fight Victoria "Posh Spice" Beckham for David Beckham?

Would you rather...

swap mothers with Lindsay Lohan

OR

swap fathers with Jessica Simpson?

YOU MUST CHOOSE!

Would you rather...

be interviewed by Oprah

OR

Ellen?

YOU MUST CHOOSE!

Who would you rather make out with?

Prince William **OR** Prince Harry?

Orlando Bloom **OR** Johnny Depp?

Brad Pitt **OR** Leonardo DiCaprio?

Follow-up: Who's your biggest celebrity crush?

YOU MUST CHOOSE!

Would you rather...

constantly be followed by Simon Cowell judging your life

OR

by Randy Jackson yelling, "Yeah, dawg!"?

Would you rather...

fall as you walk up to accept an Oscar

OR

be caught lip-synching a performance at the Grammys?

YOU MUST CHOOSE!

Would you rather...

be a backup dancer for Justin Timberlake

OR

a backup singer for Rihanna?

Would you rather...

your dad be Billy Ray Cyrus

OR

Hulk Hogan?

YOU MUST CHOOSE!

Would you rather...

have Adele's voice

OR

Jessica Alba's body?

Would you rather...

have a reality show based on your life

OR

be tracked and followed by the paparazzi?

YOU MUST CHOOSE!

Would you rather...

be the personal assistant to Mariah Carey

OR

Beyoncé?

YOU MUST CHOOSE!

Would you rather...

not wash your hair for a month to date Zac Efron

OR

eat dog food for a week to date Chace Crawford?

Would you rather...

have a celebrity alter ego (like Miley Cyrus's Hannah Montana)

OR

a super hero alter ego?

YOU MUST CHOOSE!

Would you rather...

play the love interest of Robert Pattinson in a movie

OR

record a duet with Akon on his next album?

Would you rather...

your life coach be Barack Obama

OR

Bono?

YOU MUST CHOOSE!

Would you rather...

be a Victoria's Secret model

OR

shop free at Victoria's Secret for life?

Would you rather...

be a sister to the Jonas Brothers

OR

to the Olsen twins?

YOU MUST CHOOSE!

Would you rather...

be forced to watch 24 straight hours of *The Hills*

OR

Rock of Love?

YOU MUST CHOOSE!

Would you rather...

have Madonna's arms

OR

Jessica Simpson's legs?

YOU MUST CHOOSE!

Would you rather...

your parents have named you Apple

OR

Suri?

Follow-up: What's the weirdest name you'd give a kid?

YOU MUST CHOOSE!

Would you rather...

have to clean Lindsay Lohan's house after a party

OR

organize Kimora Lee Simmons' entire closet?

YOU MUST CHOOSE!

Would you rather...

star in your high school play opposite George Clooney

OR

sing a duet in your high school talent show with John Mayer?

YOU MUST CHOOSE!

Would you rather...

be married to Gavin Rossdale

OR

Chris Martin?

YOU MUST CHOOSE!

Would you rather...

be serenaded by Jesse McCartney

OR

Jason Mraz?

YOU MUST CHOOSE!

Would you rather...

be a contestant on *Top Chef*

OR

Project Runway?

Follow-up: On what show would you most want to be a contestant?

YOU MUST CHOOSE!

Would you rather...

have the ability to stop Kanye West from speaking

OR

the ability to stop Angelina Jolie from acquiring more kids?

YOU MUST CHOOSE!

Would you rather...

star in a romantic comedy opposite Matthew McConaughey

OR

Owen Wilson?

YOU MUST CHOOSE!

Who would you rather date?

Chad Michael Murray **OR** Shane West?

Penn Badgley **OR** Ed Westwick?

Joe Jonas **OR** Nick Jonas **OR** Kevin Jonas?

YOU MUST CHOOSE!

Which celeb perk would you rather have:

personal hair and make-up artists

OR

a personal shopper?

Follow-up: What do you think would be the coolest perk to being a celebrity?

YOU MUST CHOOSE!

Thumbs Up, Thumbs Down

Circle the thumb that most reflects your feelings for each item below:

👍 👎 👎 *The Hills*

👍 👎 👎 Facebook bumper stickers

👍 👎 👎 The Bob haircut

👍 👎 👎 Uggs

👍 👎 👎 *US Weekly*

👍 👎 👎 Lady Gaga

👍 👎 👎 Greek

👍 👎 👎 *Enchanted*

👍 👎 👎 Miley Cyrus

👍 👎 👎 *I Kissed a Girl*

👍 👎 👎 Anklets

👍 👎 👎 Piercings

CHAPTER

School

School is all about answering questions. Questions on tests, questions where you're called on in class, questions about why you are forced to learn a bunch of stupid useless junk—it never seems to end. Fortunately for you, here are some questions where there are no wrong answers.

Would you rather...

be able to silence your teacher's voice at will

OR

never have to take a math class again?

Would you rather...

have your teacher be Matt Damon

OR

Seth Rogen?

Follow-up: What other star would you want as a teacher?

YOU MUST CHOOSE!

Would you rather...

take a "class" on reading celebrity gossip blogs

OR

critiquing Oscar dresses?

Follow-up: If you could take a class on anything, what would it be?

YOU MUST CHOOSE!

Would you rather...

have to go to school in a neon green wardrobe

OR

with your hair cut in the style of a mullet?

YOU MUST CHOOSE!

Would you rather...

learn Spanish in a study-abroad program in Spain

OR

from private tutoring lessons with Javier Bardem?

Would you rather...

get assigned a seat next to all the cutest guys in school

OR

be able to turn any grade into an "A"
just by blinking?

YOU MUST CHOOSE!

Would you rather...

have to be accompanied to class by your mom

OR

your brother/sister?

Would you rather...

be the class president

OR

homecoming queen?

YOU MUST CHOOSE!

Would you rather...

get paired on a class project with the most annoying kid in school

OR

your ex?

YOU MUST CHOOSE!

Would you rather...

take a dive down the stairs

OR

fart in class?

Would you rather...

get caught cheating on a test

OR

cheating on your boyfriend?

YOU MUST CHOOSE!

Would you rather...

be voted "most likely to succeed"

OR

"most popular"?

Follow-up: What "most/best" award would you like to win?

YOU MUST CHOOSE!

Would you rather...

get into the same college as your best friend

OR

your boyfriend?

Would you rather...

be the smartest girl in class

OR

the best dresser?

YOU MUST CHOOSE!

Would you rather...

your gym teacher be Tom Brady

OR

your music teacher be Justin Timberlake?

YOU MUST CHOOSE!

Would you rather...

be yearbook editor

OR

band leader?

Would you rather...

never have to study and still ace your classes

OR

never have to put in any effort and still look great?

YOU MUST CHOOSE!

Would you rather...

go to a school where you break out into musical numbers like in *High School Musical*

OR

that is full of magic like Hogwarts?

Third option: Forks High School (from *Twilight*)?

YOU MUST CHOOSE!

Would you...

cheat on a final if you knew no one would find out?

sign up for a class project with your crush if you had to do his share of the work?

try out for the football team if it got you a date with the quarterback?

YOU MUST CHOOSE!

Would you rather...

go to prom in a sweat suit

OR

go to prom with your little brother?

YOU MUST CHOOSE!

Would you rather...

attend an all-girls school

OR

a boarding school 300 miles from home?

Would you rather...

write "I will not talk in class" 500 times on the blackboard

OR

wear duct tape over your mouth all day?

YOU MUST CHOOSE!

Would you rather...

only be allowed to communicate via written notes

OR

in Pig Latin?

YOU MUST CHOOSE!

Would you rather...

be fined 50 dollars every time you swear

OR

be fined 50 dollars every time you say "like" ("I was like, then she was like..." etc.)?

YOU MUST CHOOSE!

Would you rather...

eat cafeteria food for dinner every night

OR

week-old bagels for breakfast every morning?

YOU MUST CHOOSE!

Would you rather...

spill your purse in class and have your doodles of your crush's face spill out

OR

walk around all day with your fly down?

Follow-up: What's the most embarrassing thing you've done around a boy you like?

YOU MUST CHOOSE!

Would you rather go to...

Harvard **OR** Yale?

a party college **OR** an Ivy League college?

a college in your town **OR** a college across the country?

YOU MUST CHOOSE!

Would you rather...

your high school mascot be a Chihuahua **OR** a meerkat?

a porcupine **OR** a salmon?

a toaster oven **OR** a ham and cheese sandwich?

YOU MUST CHOOSE!

Would you rather...

be the star of the basketball team

OR

the glee club?

YOU MUST CHOOSE!

Would you rather...

read your text messages aloud in class

OR

read your diary aloud in class?

YOU MUST CHOOSE!

Would you rather...

get to school via horse-drawn carriage

OR

helicopter?

YOU MUST CHOOSE!

Would you rather...

your gym uniform be a wool sweater

OR

a '70s-style leotard?

YOU MUST CHOOSE!

Would you rather...

go to school seven days a week for two hours a day

OR

two days a week for twelve hours a day?

YOU MUST CHOOSE!

CHAPTER

Friends, Frenemies and BFFs

They say you can judge a girl by the friends she keeps, but who your friends are only tells half the story. Would you throw your BFF under the bus for a boy? Do you truly prize loyalty above all else? It's time to find out where you and your best friends really stand.

Would you rather...

be BFFs with Serena van der Woodsen

OR

Blair Waldorf?

Follow-up: What fictional character do you think would make the best BFF?

YOU MUST CHOOSE!

Would you rather...

have a friend who always borrows money

OR

who always borrows your clothes, then "forgets" to return them?

YOU MUST CHOOSE!

Would you rather...

your BFF be smarter than you

OR

prettier than you?

YOU MUST CHOOSE!

Would you rather...

have to compete against your BFF for the star spot on the girls' basketball team

OR

have to compete against her for your mutual crush's affection?

YOU MUST CHOOSE!

Would you rather...

find out that your friend was dating your ex

OR

your brother?

YOU MUST CHOOSE!

Would you rather...

be equipped with a Friend Lie Detector

OR

a Boy Lie Detector?

YOU MUST CHOOSE!

Would you rather...

a frenemy write an embarrassing blog post about you

OR

post embarrassing pictures of you on Facebook?

Would you rather...

have ten casual friends

OR

one best friend?

YOU MUST CHOOSE!

Would you rather...

not be able to keep a secret

OR

not be able to tell a lie?

YOU MUST CHOOSE!

Which friend set would you rather be in?

Brains **OR** Jocks?

Band **OR** Skaters?

Preppy **OR** Punk?

YOU MUST CHOOSE!

Would you rather...

a friend tell you that your boyfriend was cheating

OR

not tell you if he was?

YOU MUST CHOOSE!

Would you rather...

have your friends and your IM conversations broadcast on TV

OR

have a really powerful microphone broadcast your conversations all day?

YOU MUST CHOOSE!

At a friend's sleepover, would you rather. . .

drool in your sleep

OR

fart in your sleep?

YOU MUST CHOOSE!

Would you rather...

have a friend who talked obsessively about her crush
(who you can't stand)

OR

physics?

YOU MUST CHOOSE!

Would you rather...

a frenemy get into your dream college

OR

date your dream guy?

YOU MUST CHOOSE!

Would you rather...

have to post a friend's bail

OR

tell her parents that she's been arrested?

Would you rather...

borrow your best friend's car and put a small scratch in it

OR

borrow her expensive new dress and rip it?

YOU MUST CHOOSE!

What's your most valued characteristic in a BFF?

loyalty **OR** honesty?

humor **OR** looks?

social status **OR** money?

YOU MUST CHOOSE!

Would you rather...

not have a single class with your BFF

OR

sit by _____ in every class?

(insert name of girl you can't stand)

YOU MUST CHOOSE!

Would you rather...

be the last of your friends to have a boyfriend

OR

the last to pass her driver's test?

YOU MUST CHOOSE!

Would you rather...

a friend copy everything you do (clothes, hair, etc.)

OR

make fun of everything you do?

YOU MUST CHOOSE!

Would you rather...

have a friend who always talked in a robot voice

OR

in IM-speak ("btw," "lol," etc.)?

YOU MUST CHOOSE!

Would you rather...

have a friend who had a mullet

OR

permanent bad breath?

YOU MUST CHOOSE!

Which celebrities would you rather be BFFs with?

Katy Perry **OR** Taylor Swift?

Tyra Banks **OR** Paris Hilton?

Anne Hathaway **OR** Kate Hudson?

YOU MUST CHOOSE!

Would you rather...

be able to magically fit into any friend's outfits

OR

be able to inflict spontaneous breakouts on girls you don't like?

YOU MUST CHOOSE!

Would you rather...

always know when people were gossiping about you

OR

only be able to hear compliments?

YOU MUST CHOOSE!

WOULD YOU RATHER BFF QUIZ

For the questions below, choose option a, b or c

1. My ideal BFF is:

    a. smart

    b. hilarious

    c. hot

2. I'd date my best friend's ex if:

    a. She said it was OK.

    b. They'd been broken up for six months.

    c. I knew she'd never find out.

3. My friends love me most because:

    a. I'm loyal.

    b. I'm a lot of fun.

    c. I'm super cute.

4. The most embarrassing thing my BFF has witnessed is:

    a. Me crying after a break-up.

    b. Me farting really loudly.

    c. Me with no makeup on.

5. The most annoying thing about being my friend is:

a. I talk too much.

b. I really like being right.

c. Please—I'm not annoying, you are.

6. The celebrity I'd probably be friends with is:

a. Jennifer Aniston

b. Jessica Simpson

c. Amy Winehouse

7. My friends make fun of me because:

    a. I'm a bookworm.

    b. I'm hopeless around guys.

    c. My clothes are too tight.

8. I'm really good at:

    a. Cheering up friends when they're upset.

    b. Giving solid advice.

    c. Everything.

9. I get mad when:

a. A friend talks behind my back.

b. My friends get together without me.

c. A friend looks better than I do.

10. I can't deal with a friend who's not:

a. trustworthy

b. fun-loving

c. popular

Mostly A's: We'd tell you all our BFF-worthy secrets.

Mostly B's: We'd definitely hang out with you.

Mostly C's: We'd rather compete to be Paris Hilton's bestie, thanks.

Would you rather...

beat out your friend to get the lead in the school play

OR

purposefully flub your audition so she'd get the part?

Would you rather...

take your BFFs on a free beach vacation

OR

get a free car?

YOU MUST CHOOSE!

Would you...

tell your BFF's biggest secret in exchange for full college tuition?

let a friend cheat off your English test if she needed an A to graduate?

skip your BFF's surprise 16th birthday party to go on a date with Zac Efron?

YOU MUST CHOOSE!

Would you rather...

lose touch with your high school friends when you got to college

OR

be friends with only your high school friends when you're 30?

YOU MUST CHOOSE!

Would you rather...

your BFF date an insufferable art student who only wanted to talk about his "vision"

OR

a creep who always hit on you—and everyone else—behind her back?

YOU MUST CHOOSE!

CHAPTER

Would You?

Sometimes, simple "yes or no" questions are the hardest. Case in point: this chapter. The questions only require a one word answer, but getting to the answer is the hard part. Should you?... Could you?... Would you?

Would you...

sleep outside for a week to go on a date with your crush?

What would you do for $1,000?

go to school dressed as Ronald McDonald?

kiss your best friend's boyfriend?

set your whole wardrobe on fire?

YOU MUST CHOOSE!

Would you...

eat nothing but tofu for a month if afterward you could have French fries at every meal and not gain weight?

Would you...

streak naked across the football field during halftime for a $10,000 shopping spree?

YOU MUST CHOOSE!

Would you...

spend two weeks locked in a room with your worst enemy to appear on the cover of *Seventeen* Magazine?

YOU MUST CHOOSE!

Would you...

dye your hair green for a year for a new car?

Would you...

give up text messaging for a year for a free trip to Paris?

Would you...

give up texting and email for the rest of your life to have a private jet?

YOU MUST CHOOSE!

Would you...

date the most annoying guy in school for two weeks to make out with James Franco?

How about...

> Drake Bell?
>
> Ed Westwick?
>
> Rupert Grint?

YOU MUST CHOOSE!

Would you...

eat a plate of deep-fried ants to get a date with Brad Pitt?

How about...

wearing the same outfit you are currently wearing every day for the next 3 months?

repeating an entire year of school?

surgically removing your pinky toe?

YOU MUST CHOOSE!

Would you...

wear diapers outside your jeans for a month to grow three inches taller?

YOU MUST CHOOSE!

Would you...

pay $1,000 for the ability to make any boy you want ask you out?

Follow-up: Would you want that same ability if it meant you had to gain 25 pounds to have that power (you wouldn't need to pay the $1,000 though)?

YOU MUST CHOOSE!

Would you...

take your little brother with you everywhere if your parents gave you a $100/week allowance?

Would you...

date the biggest geek in school if he'd help you pass physics?

YOU MUST CHOOSE!

Would you...

ever lie to your parents about where you were going to sneak out with your dream guy?

YOU MUST CHOOSE!

Would you...

chug a gallon of milk in a minute for a lifetime supply of Starbucks?

Would you...

go out with a guy with halitosis if he was a great kisser?

YOU MUST CHOOSE!

Would you...

rat out your BFF if she did something for which you were getting blamed?

Follow-up: Would you 'fess up if she were taking the rap for you?

YOU MUST CHOOSE!

129

Would you...

eat a large bowl of gravy for dinner for 30 nights to get a date with Justin Timberlake?

How about...

> hot sauce?
>
> butter?
>
> lard?

YOU MUST CHOOSE!

Would you...

want your parents to go on *What Not to Wear?*

Would you...

shower in sewer water for an hour to make out with Ryan Gosling for five minutes?

YOU MUST CHOOSE!

Would you...

use only clown makeup if doing so would mean you'd never get a zit again?

Would you...

get a permanent bright orange spray tan if you'd also get a bikini-perfect body?

YOU MUST CHOOSE!

Would you...

let your parents respond to all of your texts on your behalf if they'd pay your cell phone bills for life?

YOU MUST CHOOSE!

Would you...

date the hottest guy in school if you knew he'd cheat on you?

YOU MUST CHOOSE!

Would you...

cheat on a final if an A would get you a full college scholarship—and you had no chance of getting caught?

How about if you had...

> a 20% chance of getting caught?
>
> a 50% chance?
>
> a 75% chance?

YOU MUST CHOOSE!

Would you...

keep your BFF's biggest secret in the world if you were offered $10 million to tell?

YOU MUST CHOOSE!

Would you...

dump your boyfriend if Chace Crawford asked you out?

YOU MUST CHOOSE!

Thumbs Up, Thumbs Down

Circle the thumb that most reflects your feelings for each item below:

👍 👎 👎 Terrycloth pants

👍 👎 👎 Limited Too

👍 👎 👎 Dramatic chip-munk (on YouTube)

👍 👎 👎 Britney Spears

👍 👎 👎 Twilight

👍 👎 👎 Abrevs

👍 👎 👎 Blake Lively

👍 👎 👎 John Mayer

👍 👎 👎 Tyra Banks

👍 👎 👎 Leggings

👍 👎 👎 Myspace

👍 👎 👎 Bottled water

CHAPTER

Getting personal

It's time to get personal! Challenge your friends with these personalized puzzlers involving people you know and love (and hate.)

Would you rather...

spend 5 hours in a car with _____
(insert incredibly annoying acquaintance)

OR

be stuck in an elevator for 10 hours with _____ ?
(insert acquaintance with terrible hygiene)

Would you rather...

make out with _____
(insert geekiest guy in school)

OR

be publicly dumped by _____ ?
(insert hottest guy in school)

YOU MUST CHOOSE!

Would you rather...

fall down the stairs in front of _____
(insert crush's name)

OR

get caught making out with a guy in front of _____ ?
(insert teacher's name)

Would you rather...

walk in on _____ making out
(insert family members)

OR

walk in on _____ making out?
(insert two gross people)

YOU MUST CHOOSE!

Would you rather...

have the hair of _____
(insert schoolmate with bad hair)

OR

wear the same clothes as _____ ?
(insert schoolmate with awful style)

Would you rather...

get into a shouting match with _____
(insert girl friend)

OR

an actual fight with _____ ?
(insert girl friend)

YOU MUST CHOOSE!

Would you rather...

share a dorm room with _____
(insert messiest friend)

OR

share clothes with _____ ?
(insert worst-dressed friend)

YOU MUST CHOOSE!

Would you rather...

read _____ for 5 hours
(insert boring textbook)

OR

watch _____ for 10 hours?
(insert mindless reality TV show)

Would you rather...

listen to every song on _____ 's iPod
(insert lame acquaintance)

OR

every song by _____ ?
(insert bad band)

YOU MUST CHOOSE!

Would you rather...

be a taste-tester for _____
(insert favorite restaurant)

OR

a fashion tester for _____ ?
(insert favorite brand)

YOU MUST CHOOSE!

Would you rather...

be able to get a higher grade than _____
(insert smartest classmate)

OR

be able to date _____ ?
(insert cutest classmate)

Would you rather...

be able to change the appearance of your _____
(insert body part)

OR

magically become a size _____ ?
(insert clothing size)

YOU MUST CHOOSE!

Would you rather...

wear 10 pounds of _____
(insert accessory)

OR

have to go without _____ ?
(insert article of clothing)

YOU MUST CHOOSE!

Would you rather...

win a free vacation to _____
(insert location)

OR

never have to pay for _____ again?
(insert noun)

Would you rather...

share your e-mails with _____
(insert family member)

OR

share your boyfriend with _____?
(insert girl friend)

YOU MUST CHOOSE!

Would you rather...

arrive at school in a _____
(insert emergency vehicle)

OR

on a _____?
(insert animal)

YOU MUST CHOOSE!

Would you rather...

instantly be able to speak perfect _____
(insert foreign language)

OR

spend a month in _____ ?
(insert foreign country)

YOU MUST CHOOSE!

Would you rather...

wash your hair with _____
(insert liquid)

OR

cut your nails with _____ ?
(insert sharp object)

YOU MUST CHOOSE!

Insert three female celebrities:

_____

_____

_____

Who would you rather...

Go shopping with?

Look like?

Get into a fight with?

YOU MUST CHOOSE!

Insert three male celebrities:

_____

_____

_____

Who would you rather...

Marry?

Date?

Make out with?

YOU MUST CHOOSE!

153

Would you rather...

star on _____
(insert TV show)

OR

live next door to _____ ?
(insert celebrity)

Would you rather...

have _____
(insert magical power)

OR

_____ ?
(insert dollar amount)

YOU MUST CHOOSE!

Would you rather...

lose your mom's favorite _____
(insert jewelry)

OR

ruin your dad's _____ ?
(insert favorite thing)

YOU MUST CHOOSE!

155

Would you give up _____ for...

(insert prized possession)

a new car?

a trip to Italy?

perfect hair?

YOU MUST CHOOSE!

Would you rather...

eat only _____
(insert candy)

OR

drink only _____ ?
(insert beverage)

Would you rather...

go back to age _____
(insert younger age)

OR

skip ahead to age _____ ?
(insert older age)

YOU MUST CHOOSE!

Would you rather...

be handcuffed to _____ for a week
(insert annoying acquaintance)

OR

not be able to talk to _____ for a month?
(insert good friend)

Would you rather...

have a potion that repelled _____ guys
(insert adjective)

OR

a potion that attracted _____ guys?
(insert adjective)

YOU MUST CHOOSE!

Would you rather...

be able to _____
(insert talent)

OR

_____ ?
(insert super-hero power)

YOU MUST CHOOSE!

159

Would you rather...

smell like _____ no matter how much you showered
(insert foul odor)

OR

have a permanent zit on your _____ ?
(insert body part/facial feature)

Would you rather...

sleep on a bed of _____
(insert hard object)

OR

have to share a bed with _____ ?
(insert unappealing person)

YOU MUST CHOOSE!

Would you rather...

rip your _____ in the middle of class
(insert article of clothing)

OR

fall asleep in class and _____ in your sleep?
(insert verb)

YOU MUST CHOOSE!

Would you rather...

be dared to tell _____ that you love them
                        (insert person)

OR

have to tell the story of _____ in front of the
                          (insert embarrassing moment)
whole school?

Would you rather...

have a boyfriend who only wore _____
                                (insert bad fashion choice)

OR

who was terrible at _____ ?
                    (insert activity)

YOU MUST CHOOSE!

Would you rather...

date _____
(insert male celebrity)

OR

look like _____ ?
(insert female celebrity)

YOU MUST CHOOSE!

Would you rather...

gain _____ pounds freshman year of college

(insert number)

OR

your nose grow _____ ?

(insert length)

YOU MUST CHOOSE!

Instead of detention, would you rather your punishment be...

spending a week with _____
(insert obnoxious classmate)

OR

going on a date with _____ ?
(insert unattractive guy)

YOU MUST CHOOSE!

CHAPTER

Random Play

You've handled all the tough questions and quandaries so far.
But now, you have no idea what to expect....

Would you rather...

be able to burp the alphabet

OR

play "Happy Birthday" with your armpit?

Would you rather...

speak in tongues when you're nervous

OR

projectile vomit?

YOU MUST CHOOSE!

Would you rather...

have an infinite wardrobe

OR

an infinite allowance?

YOU MUST CHOOSE!

Would you rather...

give up your cell phone

OR

your computer?

YOU MUST CHOOSE!

Would you rather...

have glue-tipped fingers

OR

pogo-stick feet?

YOU MUST CHOOSE!

Would you rather... BFF

Would you rather...

brush your teeth with dishwashing liquid

OR

wash your hair with laundry detergent?

Would you rather...

date a guy with a third eye

OR

an impenetrably thick coat of back hair?

YOU MUST CHOOSE!

Would you rather...

have supernatural hearing

OR

x-ray vision?

Things to consider: Gossip, the boxers-or-briefs debate

YOU MUST CHOOSE!

Would you rather...

share bunk beds with your brattiest sibling

OR

share a bathroom with the entire guys' basketball team?

Would you rather...

face Simon on *American Idol*

OR

break your ankle on *Dancing with the Stars*?

YOU MUST CHOOSE!

What would you do for a date with Robert Pattinson?

Go without sleep for three days?

Make monkey noises instead of speaking for a week?

Give up a month's allowance?

YOU MUST CHOOSE!

175

Would you rather...

have everything you do automatically Twittered

OR

automatically texted to your parents' cell phones?

Would you rather...

eat a peanut-butter-and-chicken-liver sandwich

OR

drink a raw-egg-and-hot-sauce milkshake?

Follow-up: What's the grossest thing you ever consumed?

YOU MUST CHOOSE!

Would you rather...

win $1 million

OR

spend one week on a desert island with your crush?

YOU MUST CHOOSE!

Would you rather...

wear garlic-scented perfume

OR

mushroom-flavored lip gloss?

Would you rather...

cut a guy's lip with your braces during a kiss

OR

accidentally bite his tongue?

YOU MUST CHOOSE!

Would you rather...

have rapidly growing leg hair

OR

hair growing out of your ears?

YOU MUST CHOOSE!

Would you rather...

get locked in the mall after closing time

OR

be stuck on the ferris wheel at an amusement park after closing time?

YOU MUST CHOOSE!

Would you rather...

your crush study with you for a big test

OR

be able to learn everything just by sleeping with the textbook under your pillow?

YOU MUST CHOOSE!

Would you rather...

your boyfriend have a collection of Beanie Babies

OR

tattoos?

Would you rather...

always get A's without ever having to study

OR

have a great body without ever having
to diet?

YOU MUST CHOOSE!

Would you rather...

break up with your boyfriend in the hallway between classes

OR

via text message?

YOU MUST CHOOSE!

About the Author

Courtney Balestier is a writer and editor thrilled to finally have a shame-free outlet for her *Gossip Girl* obsessions. When she's not wondering how Blair Waldorf's headband stays in place or why Chuck Bass speaks in a permanent whisper, Courtney can be found writing, talking or thinking about food and music, though not necessarily together. (Luckily, she has found publications willing to publish her work that don't frown upon such behavior.) Courtney lives in Brooklyn, by way of Morgantown, West Virginia.

Because everyone has an opinion...
there's a *Would You Rather...?* title for everyone!

The media obsessed:

People who can't get enough of a good thing:

The romantically-inclined:

People who REALLY can't get enough of a good thing:

People on the go:

People who REALLY REALLY can't get enough of a good thing:

People who prefer pictures to words:

All kids:

People obsessed with money:

All kids, but mostly boys:

www.wouldyourather.com

www.sevenfooterpress.com